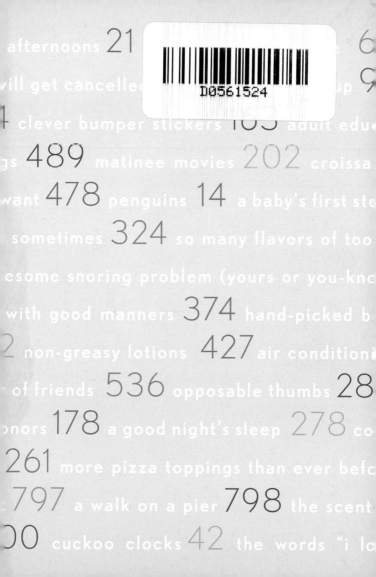

afternoons 21

will get cancelle... D0561524 ...up 9

clever bumper stickers 103 adult edu...

gs 489 matinee movies 202 croissa...

want 478 penguins 14 a baby's first ste...

sometimes 324 so many flavors of too...

esome snoring problem (yours or you-kno...

with good manners 374 hand-picked b...

2 non-greasy lotions 427 air conditioni...

of friends 536 opposable thumbs 28...

onors 178 a good night's sleep 278 co...

261 more pizza toppings than ever befo...

797 a walk on a pier 798 the scent...

00 cuckoo clocks 42 the words "i lo...

for JAKE
from ANGELL

Published by Hallmark Books,
a division of Hallmark Cards, Inc.,
Kansas City, MO 64141
Visit us on the Web at www.Hallmark.com.

Editorial Director: Todd Hafer
Art Director: Kevin Swanson
Designer: Mary Eakin
Production Artist: Dan Horton

ISBN: 978-1-59530-011-9

BOK6086

Printed and bound in China

GIFT BOOKS
from Hallmark

1001
things to be
thankful for

"gratitude
is the key to happiness."

C.S. LEWIS

1

the first daffodils
of spring

2

a smile from a stranger

3

more tv channels = more choices

4

blueberry scones

5

low-fat ice cream

6

friends who believe in you

7

the chance to give to a favorite charity
"to be able to find joy in another's joy,
that is the secret of happiness."
GEORGE BERNANOS

8

love notes

9

art museums

10

satellite radio

11

the smell of fresh-cut timber

12

deep roots

13

morning dew

14

a baby's first steps

15

crisp autumn air

16

family game night

17

jack-o'-lanterns

18

secret santas

19
rocking chairs

20
pecan pie

21
music in the distance

22
the first juicy bite of an apple

23
steel-cut oatmeal

24
a field of wildflowers

25
text messaging

26
lavender hand cream

27
guitar solos

28
anonymous donors

29
the bill of rights

30
shampoo and conditioner in one bottle

31
miles davis

32
buttered toast

33
hot-fudge sundaes

34
juicy plums

35
"charlotte's web"

36
cornfields

37
fall leaves

38
the wind in the wheat

39
well-marked roads

40
wise words

41
emergency call boxes

42
the words "i love you" never get old

43
running shoes look cooler than ever

44
the familiar scents of home

45
independent films

46

wind in your sails (literally or metaphorically)

47

live music

48

funnel cake

49

bugs bunny

50

marvel comics

51

mac and cheese with real cheese

52

a friendly flight attendant

53

smooth landings

54

photo albums

⁵⁵ jugglers

56
beach volleyball,
whether a spectator or a player

57
homemade jam

58
the welcoming glow
of a porch light

59
leap years

60
museums of natural history

61
reliable baby-sitters

62
cancelled business meetings
"what the world really needs is more love
and less paperwork."
PEARL BAILEY

63
computers keep getting cheaper, lighter, and faster

64
department-store santas

65
freedom
"the secret of happiness"
THUCYDIDES

66
the declaration of independence

67
freshly ironed clothes

68
there's always a chance
that boring seminar will get cancelled

69
video-store late fees are becoming extinct

70
rumble strips

state fairs

72
johnny cash compilations

73
black-and-white movies
on late-night tv

74
rock 'n' roll reunion tours

75
classic disney flicks

76
a tail-wagging greeting
from a dog

77
indie record labels

78
pure maple syrup

79
superstar athletes who still
sign autographs – for free

80

martin luther king jr.'s "i have a dream" speech

81

beethoven symphonies

82

home-canned vegetables

83

window shopping

84

texas toast

85

hot tubs

86

drum solos

87

exercise dvds

88

waking up to a brand-new day

89
the simpsons...
still funny after all these years

90
the north star

91
fond good-bye waves

92
all of those flavored coffee creamers

93
the privilege of reading to a child
"when i grow up, i want to be a little boy."
JOSEPH HELLER

94
more soda flavors than ever before

95
the healthful powers of pomegranate juice

96
large-print books

97
pedicures

98
souvenir t-shirts

99
peppermint bark

100
vintage sepia photographs

101
stretch denim

102
canada geese in flight

103
a brightly lit christmas tree

104
meerkats

105
history books

106
sunlight filling up a favorite room

107
ken burns films

108
a perfect tennis partner

109
you can create your own web site

110
national public radio

111
high-definition tv

112
full-service gas stations

113
goodnight kisses

114
multi-grain bread

115
red wine is good
for you

116
calculators

117
starving-artist exhibits
"beauty comes in all ages, colors,
shapes, and forms."
KATHY IRELAND

118
small-town newspapers

119
a fish at the end of your line

120
free parking

121
dark chocolate is good for you

122
fresh, homemade salsa

123
pixar movies

124

good-flavored mouthwash

125

super bowl parties

126

high-flying kites

127

cinnamon toast

128

lemon laws

129

merry-go-rounds

130

breakfast in bed

131

almond butter

132

march madness

133
cotton candy

134
college radio stations

135
fantasy football leagues

136
finding your groove from the free-throw line

137
an unexpectedly warm winter day

138
smooth, cool sheets
on a hot summer night

139
you eventually grow out of
a bad haircut

140
open-mike night
at the comedy club

141
your favorite musical

142
winnie the pooh

143
funny t-shirts

144
great books that become great movies

145
bicycle rides

146
nature preserves

147
hikes in the woods

148
back rubs

149
best-seller lists

150
small-college basketball

151
small-college football

152
romantic picnics

153
fresh peaches

154
clever bumper stickers

155
having a favorite song
as your ring-tone

156
restaurants that stay
open late

157
bird feeders

158
undrafted, unheralded athletes who
make it to the pros

159
drive-through windows

160
playing footsie

161
slow drives down a country road

162
receiving a hand-written
love letter

163
adult education classes

164
omelets

165
hot, cheesy pizza

roller
coasters

167

manicures

168

noble douglas fir trees

169

spring is never that far away

170

high school football games

171

saturday morning cartoons

172

green tea

173

dvds with all those extra features

174

a cool glass of water

175

state wrestling tournaments

176
small mistakes, which save you
from making bigger ones later on
"mistakes are a fact of life. it's
the response to the error that counts."
NIKKI GIOVANNI

177
a family who believes in you

178
a good night's sleep

179
baseball players who always
run hard to first base

180
academic all-americans

181
tire swings

182
flags on the 4th of july

183
morning mist

184
toast that falls jam-side-up

185
your signature looks cool!

186
a challenging sudoku puzzle—
but not too challenging

187
"banker's hours" are now more
like everyone else's hours

188
a game of backyard touch football

189
the simple charm of daisies

190
foot rubs

191
homemade fudge

192
cranberry juice

193
the aroma of fresh coffee in the morning

194
guacamole

195
piano recitals

196
clouds brushing past a full moon

197
dollar stores

198
a day of mail with no bills

199
trickling brooks

200
the soothing warmth of a loving hand

201
there is always something new to learn
"the important thing is to never stop questioning."

ALBERT EINSTEIN

202
croissants

203
a beckoning mountain trail

204
ice packs

205
crocuses in bloom

206
a walk along a country road

207
donut holes

208
birds singing in the morning
"the music soars within
the little lark, and the lark soars."
ELIZABETH BARRETT BROWNING

209
pleasant dreams

210
a shoulder to cry on

211
the first page of a new book

212
turns out that eggs aren't
really bad for you

213
you can now record favorite tv shows
and watch them whenever

214
you don't live in the
pre-dishwasher era

215
a good movie
on a rainy afternoon

216
you look a lot better than
that celebrity who just had more
plastic surgery

217
curiosity
"give curiosity freedom."
EUDORA WELTY

218
generosity
"dear god, teach us to share
with others what we ourselves have."
CHINESE CHILDREN'S PRAYER

219
delegating

220
used-book stores

221
frozen double mocha
peppermint lattes
(with skim milk,
of course)

222
friday is never that far away

223
john hughes movies

224
a bouquet of fresh flowers

225
s'mores

226
a mailbox full of catalogs you actually want

227
online bill pay

228
cuddling

229
dance recitals

230
heat packs

231
the underdog still wins sometimes

232
seashells

233
garage sales

234
fresh-squeezed lemonade

235
even mcdonald's has some healthful
stuff on the menu

236
some really good allergy medicines
are now available over-the-counter

237
the newspaper funny pages

238
dogs who fetch

239

burning your own cds –
or having a techie friend do it for you

240

maya angelou's poetry

241

puppies

242

eva cassidy collections

243

reaching a milestone

244

movies with surprise endings

245

movies with happy endings

246

a barista who makes your
cappuccino just perfectly

247
uncomfortable shoes are
OUT

248

overdraft protection

249

the kindness of strangers

250

spam filters

251

"to kill a mockingbird" (the book and the movie)

252

tickle fights

253

kindergarten teachers

254

candlelight dinners

255

sunrises
"may the great mystery
make sunrise in your heart."
SIOUX INDIAN BLESSING

256
daydreams
"a man is not old until regrets
take the place of dreams."
JOHN BARRYMORE

257
hearing "i'm sorry"

258
100% juice

259
butterflies

260
a big dessert...and two spoons

261
more pizza toppings than ever before

262
the world is still filled with wonder

263
grace periods

264
hayrides

265
most elevators don't play music anymore

266
personal address labels

267
somebody has a crush on you—
maybe even a few "somebodies"

268
warm spring days

269
there's a lot of cool exercise
equipment for the home

270
your car's fuel gauge

271
bubble gum is still fun –
and still cheap

272
boat rides

273
our brave men and women in the military

274
stevie wonder

275
an honest day's work

276
bubble baths

277
thunderstorms

278
compliments

279
jigsaw puzzles

280
a few minutes of quiet time

281
bargain bookstores

282
your imagination

283
there's almost always a "seinfeld" rerun on

284
eyeglasses are in – and there's a style
that will look great on you

285
hello, national do-not-call list;
good-bye, telemarketers

286
high school musicals

287
new acquaintances who pronounce
your name right – the first time

288
getting someone's autograph

289
quiet mornings
(rare though they might be)

290
naps are in (call yours a "power nap"
if it makes you feel better)
"no day is so bad that it can't be
fixed with a nap."
CARRIE SNOW

291
decaf coffee

292
laughing until your sides hurt

293
hot-air balloons

294
tiny paper umbrellas

295
goldfish crackers

296
oprah's book club

297
watching the tide come in

298
sunscreen

299
do-it-yourself television shows

300
sports mascots

301
volunteers
"if your experiences would
benefit anybody, give them
to someone."
FLORENCE NIGHTINGALE

302
a challenging crossword puzzle
(but not too challenging)

303
surprise
parties

304

toasted bagels with
cream cheese

305

a really good piece
of key lime pie

306

james taylor

307

hot apple cider

308

second-hand clothing shops

309

picking your own pumpkin

310

homecomings

311

learning to play chess

312
dr. seuss books

313
the memory of your first kiss

314
cameron crowe movies
(except "vanilla sky," of course)

315
it takes 26 muscles to smile;
just think of the workout you'll get
when you're happy

316
fresh-squeezed orange juice

317
automated car washes –
part labor-saving convenience,
part amusement-park ride

318
road trips with friends

319
when someone you love
makes the honor roll

320
hearing your favorite song on the radio

321
baby-sitters are still reasonably priced

322
a favorite movie
just released on dvd

323
a night out with friends

324
so many flavors of toothpaste

325
they didn't make a sequel to "casablanca"

326
there's some loose cash lurking somewhere
in your home; you'll find it, eventually

327
there are more coffee flavors than ever -
even for people who don't like coffee

328
they've finally created some energy bars
that don't taste like cardboard

329
books are still one of the best bargains around

330
fresh-fruit smoothies

331
cinnamon apples

332
wikipedia

333
google earth

334
homemade mashed potatoes

335
roasted pumpkin seeds

336
spell-check

337
grammar-check

338
bubble wrap is fun to pop

339
the distant cry of a train whistle

340
disposable contact lenses

341
milk duds are low-fat

342
re-gifting is still socially acceptable
if you're discreet

343
when your home team wins a big game

344
free samples

345
you're probably better at ping pong
than you think

346
flavored dental floss

347
the kids in your life like dylan and
zeppelin as much as you do

348
that thing you've been
trying to recall? don't worry;
it'll come back to you

349
homemade pumpkin pie

350
hitting all the
green lights

351

young children with good manners

352

teenagers with good manners

353

all kinds of ipods

354

saltwater taffy is delicious
(and doesn't actually taste salty)

355

sugar-free jams and preserves

356

your favorite team will have a
better season next year

357

that pasteurized egg stuff means worry-free
cake-batter and cookie-dough eating

358

accordions

359
you may still have some sick days left

360
check your calendar; there's a three-day
weekend coming up

361
improv comedians

362
self-cleaning ovens

363
bob dylan

364
van morrison

365
a moment of epiphany

366
hybrid vehicles
are getting cheaper

367

watching hummingbirds do their thing

368

your hair looks way, way
better than donald trump's

369

free refills

370

the really big
box of crayons

371

people who adopt animal-shelter pets

372

"the office" on dvd

373

alternative energy

374

hand-picked berries

375
you could be eating hot popcorn
in about five minutes

376
the johnny carson-era
"tonight show" on dvd

377
bedtime stories – whether you're
the reader or the audience

378
caller i.d.

379
girl scout cookies

380
being prepared

381
digital cameras

382
the sound of a cat purring

383
cuddling

384
your mail carrier

385
fancy little soaps

386
a great hair day

387
flannel sheets

388
mini marshmallows

389
room service

390
sporks

391
lighthouses

392
a game of catch

393
barbecue sauce

394
wedding anniversaries

395
slow dancing

396
there are seven wonders of the world,
not a mere five or six

397
"peanuts" comics
and tv specials

398
babies seem to like you

399
any opportunity to sleep in

400
lots of remedies for that
troublesome snoring problem
(yours or you-know-whose)

401
a good set of tools

402
non-greasy lotions

403
chili cook-offs

404
postage-paid return envelopes

405
classic grace kelly movies

406
ladybugs

407
you don't have to pretend to like
foreign films if you really don't

408 gumballs

409
mozart's music

410
chivalry isn't dead –
and you can keep encouraging it

411
marx brothers movies

412
birthday cake

413
shakespeare
"oh lord, that lends me life,
lend me a heart replete
with thankfulness."
WILLIAM SHAKESPEARE

414
birthday parties

415
the national anthem

416
turkey bacon

417
nutritional labels

418
ansel adams photography

419
that tv show that always annoyed you
is probably about to get cancelled

420
"sportscenter" is on multiple times every day

421
you can make your hair pretty much
any color you want

422
stephen colbert

423
that anti-baldness stuff is now
available over the counter

424
bendy straws

425
when your server asks,
"would you like fresh-grated
parmesan on that?"

426
a bowl of chili on a frozen day

427
air conditioning

428
the beatles

429
luggage on wheels

430
rainy-day puddle-splashing

431
"america the beautiful"

432
the all-natural runner's high

433
books on tape, cd, and online

434
celebrity gossip

435
cherry blossoms

436
a blended family that really blends

437
peach cobbler

438
sinatra ballads

439
a place to put your feet up

440
the abundance of fat-free snacks

441
frequent-flier miles

442
four-day weekends

443
bogart movies

444
free cell phone minutes

445
a game of checkers with a worthy foe

446
romance isn't dead

447
a fresh, crisp salad

448
new shoes

449
adversity makes for a great education

450
steaks sizzling on a grill

451
knowing more than a game-show contestant

452
the rolling stones are still making music
(and it's still pretty good)

453
those cholesterol-lowering
medications really work

454
red beans and rice

455
snapdragons

456
goldfinches

457
advance reservations

458
a really intriguing mystery

459
wind chimes

460
homemade chicken noodle soup

461
counting stars at night

462
the laughter of friends

463
hiking trails

464
wedding bells

465
reserved seating

466
steve mcqueen flicks

467

the first day of vacation

468

miniature golf

469

gentle rain

470

"my so-called life" on dvd

471

fine wine

472

free chips with your sandwich

473

knock-knock jokes

474

sunrise

475

porch swings

476
hammocks

477
"mythbusters"

478
penguins

479
common sense

480
a really good batch
of french fries

481
gentle reminders

482
indian-summer days

483
sending that slow softball pitch
into deep, deep center field

484
lunch
hour

485

that new issue of your favorite
magazine will be in your mailbox -
or on the newsstand - soon

486

peace treaties

487

there are no failures - only learners
"the years teach much which the
days never know."

RALPH WALDO EMERSON

488

bake sales

489

matinee movies

490

cinnamon sugar

491

a bandage where it hurts

492
a kiss where it hurts

493
grandparents

494
little league baseball games

495
party hats

496
family picnics

497
classic black-and-white
horror films

498
a fresh danish with your
morning coffee

499
doing good...and feeling good

500
adoptive parents

501
choices

502
new-baby announcements

503
baby pictures

504
apple blossoms

505
slow walks in the park

506
a big bowl of wiggly jell-o

507
family traditions

508
fresh donuts

509

louis armstrong's version of
"what a wonderful world"

510

the power of prayer
"courage is fear that has said its prayers."
DOROTHY BERNARD

511

christmas lights

512

rainbows

513

fishing with buddies

514

aging with grace
"fortunate are those
who actually enjoy old age."
JEWISH PROVERB

515

"the far side"

516
daylight savings time

517
warm mittens

518
mood lighting

519
there will be some great pictures
on that old roll of undeveloped
film you just found

520
waterproof mascara

521
you don't have to eat liver ever again –
unless you want to

522
rice krispie treats

523
roadside fruit-and-vegetable stands

524
fresh mozzarella cheese

525
comfort food

526
blueberries: not just
a delicious fruit,
but an antioxidant too!

527
warm, fluffy clothes and towels
fresh from the dryer

528
moist towlettes

529
one benefit to not being a baby:
when you smile, no one surmises,
"it's probably just gas"

530
cherry cough drops

531
even water comes in a variety of flavors now

532
dressing up

533
finishing a 5k

534
a good, soul-cleansing cry

535
lessons learned – even the hard ones
"if you want the rainbow,
you gotta put up with the rain."
DOLLY PARTON

536
opposable thumbs

537
aids research

538
rest stops

539
snickerdoodles

540
hope still happens
"it's so important to know that you can
choose to feel good. most people don't
think they have that choice."
NEIL SIMON

541
vegetarian pizza

542
judy garland's version of
"somewhere over the rainbow"

543
moonlit walks

544
hello kisses

545
jelly beans

546
advances in cancer treatment

547
charity car washes

548
tailgating before the big game

549
award banquets

550
motorcycle
rides

551
horse-drawn carriages

552
summer camp

553
stories around a campfire

554
songs around a campfire
"you are happiest when you make your own
music your own way."
LINDA BARNES

555
chunky peanut butter

556
smooth peanut butter

557
a cup of tea and a quiet moment

558
old friends

559
new friends

560
christmas carolers

561
your memories –
your own private literature

562
vegetable gardens

563
ice cream cones

564
flower gardens

565
really good coffee cake at the
office morning meeting

566
a bowl of fresh fruit

567
cool grass under your bare feet

568
hot chocolate with marshmallows

569
dave barry's writing

570
getting the new book by your favorite author

571
sun-dried tomatoes

572
wedding pictures

573
discovering a new comedian
who's genuinely funny

574
street-corner musicians
"i merely took the energy it takes to pout
and wrote some blues."
DUKE ELLINGTON

575
cup holders

576
clouds that look like animals

577
good-bye kisses

578
an itch you can actually reach

579
pants that fit

580
snowball fights

581
your favorite hobby

582
courteous drivers

583
the smell (and taste) of freshly
baked chocolate chip cookies

584
being able
to admit you're wrong

585
a good old, loyal dog

586
a hand to hold

587
soothing incense

588
a hug when you really need it

589
flea markets

590
banana splits

591
classical guitar music

592
the spring breeze coming
through an open window

593
siblings

594
watching the seasons change

595
the look of wonder
in a child's eyes

596
homemade potato salad

597
takeout chinese food

598
snow angels

599
homemade fried chicken

600
a seemingly infinite supply
of james bonds

601
finding cash in a coat pocket

602
recycling centers

603
a restaurant where they know you by name

604
those bleak weather forecasts
are wrong sometimes

605
take-and-bake pizza

606
perfection is overrated

607
summer vacations

608
bake-offs

609
skipping stones

610
sunday drives

611
eggnog

612
a sharp pencil and a clean sheet of paper
"art is the only way to run
away without leaving home."
TWYLA THARP

613
a comfortable chair

614
the headlights in the
driveway that mean
someone special is home

615
bach fugues

616
route 66

617
fresh biscuits

618
someone to tuck in at night

619
the wisdom of growing older

620
waterproof clothing

621
banana bread

622
a child's artwork

623
housework burns 250 calories per hour

624
fire fighters

625
pens with erasers

626
that new-baby smell

627
baby steps

628
falling into bed after a long, productive day
"a well-spent day means happy sleep."
LEONARDO DA VINCI

629
wet sand under your bare feet

630
getting a birthday card

631
a moment of silence

632
getting a smile from a baby

633
iced tea on a hot day

634
getting a letter or e-mail from an old friend

635
tv dinners

636
low-fat hot dogs

637
clear, starry nights

638
the downtown diner

639
sugar cookies made with real butter

640
fireflies twinkling on a dark night

641
movie theater candy

642
an old-fashioned family dinner

643
the family dog

644
the family cat

645
midnight snacks

646
open-all-night convenience stores

647
your neighborhood police officers

648
whole-wheat toast with butter and honey

649

your local search and rescue

650

freshly baked bread

651

lifeguards

652

cpr

653

lazy summer afternoons

654

barefoot walks

655

badminton

656

anything cooked on a campfire

657

a breathtaking view

658
medication for high blood pressure

659
24-hour customer service

660
refrigerator magnets

661
crossing guards

662
the courage of conviction
"one man with courage makes a majority."
ANDREW JACKSON

663
sidewalk sales

664
pumpkin bread

665
role models

666
blood donors

667
tutors

668
the mute button

669
free wi-fi

670
snow globes

671
pinwheels

672

gps devices

673

first-aid kits

674

flashlights

675

self-control

676

duct tape

677

teflon

678

the right to vote

679

simon and garfunkel

680

john steinbeck

681
toni morrison

682
jane austen

683
william faulkner

684
feodor dostoevsky

685
the bronte sisters

686
a good daily planner

687
ramen noodles

688
foreign-exchange students

689
fly-fishing

690
cross-country skiing

691
online check-in

692
flu shots

693
ellis island

694
waterfalls

695
music boxes

696
insect repellant

697
suntan lotion

698
forgiveness

699
compassion

700
habitat for humanity

701
virus blockers

702
family trees

703
second chances

704
savings accounts

705
free concerts

706
compound interest

707
monday night football

708
the frozen four hockey tournament

709
a good watchdog

710
veterinarians

711
your local hospice

712
olympic medal ceremonies

713
olive oil

714
hot pretzels

715
salted peanuts

716
energy drinks

717
solar power

718
wool socks in winter

719
your favorite jeans

720
comfortable slippers

721
brad bird movies

722
"freaks and geeks" on dvd

723
mother teresa quotes

724
ergonomic furniture

725
block parties

726
family-style restaurants

727
"a prairie home companion"

728
christmas letters

729
microfiber clothing

730
unicef

731
calvin and hobbes

732
first communions

733
godparents

734
aunts and uncles

735

genealogies

736

coupons

737

classified ads

738

charming foreign accents

739

a budget you can stick to

740

microwave ovens

741

grilled-cheese sandwiches

742

farmers

743

freshness dates

744
calamine lotion

745
meteor showers

746
science fairs

747
word-search puzzles

748
antique shops

749
"it's a wonderful life"

750
"12 angry men"

751
good stationery

752
custom cds

753

farmers markets

754
the versatile potato

755
trail mix

756
tagless t-shirts

757
natural-food shops

758
pasteurization

759
michelangelo

760
"the seven habits of highly effective people"

761
mister rogers

762
snow tires

763
wherever home is

764
instruction manuals

765
talcum powder

766
spare keys

767
delayed gratification

768
firm handshakes

769
eye contact

770
professional tax assistance

771
the kelley blue book

772
carfax

773
3 x 5 index cards

774
the heimlich maneuver

775
second helpings

776
thank-you cards
"thou that hast given so much to me,
give me one thing more, a grateful heart."
GEORGE HERBERT

777
a good filing system

778
fabric softener

779
scrabble

780
bran

781
digital cameras

782
fix-a-flat in a can

783
deodorant

784
sea horses

785
eclipses

786
telescopes

787
sign language

788
your bff

789
helmets
(bicycle, motorcycle, football,
and all the rest)

790
ghost stories around a campfire

791
pizza delivery

792
bird houses

793
sandcastles

794
a nap with your pet

795
inner peace
"it is not how much we have, but how much
we enjoy, that makes happiness."

C H SPURGEON

796
sesame street

797
a walk on a pier

798
the scent of a pine forest

799
grandfather clocks

800
cuckoo clocks

801
kiwi fruit

802
the russian novelists

803
bono

804
a sturdy (but comfortable) pair of boots

805
miniature trains

806
book groups

807
happy endings

808
gingerbread men

809
giggle fits

810
waffles

811
holiday movies

812
handmade gifts
"god gave me my gifts. i will do all i can to
show him how grateful i am to him."
GRACE LIVINGSTON HILL

813
peanut butter and jelly sandwiches

814
warm cornbread

815
swimming pools

816
a timely piece of advice

817
flaxseed

818
money-back guarantees

819
"the honeymooners" reruns

820
wishing stars

821
air purifiers

822
ronald mcdonald house charities

823
chai tea

824
electric toothbrushes

825
stretchy pants

826
brown rice

827
baking soda

828
classic-car sightings

829
instant cell-phone chargers

830
soy milk

831
risotto

832
room for improvement

833
an electrical outlet where you really need one

834
cranberries

835
the office candy dish

836
life preservers

837
almonds

838
a good hand-mixer

839
waterproof matches

840

winter gardens

841

realistic expectations

842

peacemakers

843

flexibility (all kinds)

844

good neighbors

845

"no assembly required"

846

emily dickinson's poetry

847

kind words
"always be kinder than necessary."
SIR JAMES BARRIE

848
a balanced checkbook

849
lullabies

850
making footprints in the snow

851
"tuesdays with morrie"

852
recess

853
automatic doors

854
timeless songs

855
ranchers

856
honeybees

857
the changing seasons

858
watching nightfall from your front porch

859
coffee breaks

860
simple pleasures

861
travel sizes

862
chewable vitamins

863
hot oatmeal with brown sugar

864
self-awareness

865
girls' (or guys') night out

866

ordering in

867

do-not-disturb signs

868

a soothing bath

869

scented sachets

870

french toast

871

rules

872

constructive criticism

873

atm machines

874

a certificate of deposit

875
your favorite pillow

876

retirement accounts

877

rowboats

878

kites

879

your public library

880

a hand-written letter

881

wash-and-wear clothes

882

gore-tex

883

historical landmarks

884

alternate routes

885
shortcuts

886
the enduring echo of affirming words
"the best and most beautiful things
in the world cannot be seen or
even touched. they must be felt
with the heart."
HELEN KELLER

887
old photos

888
serendipity

889
humility

890
toll-free numbers

891
"never needs ironing!"

892
community theater

893
a helping hand

894
centenarians

895
nba stars who can actually
make free throws

896
home gyms

897
family recipes

898
"i love lucy"

899
meals on wheels

900
food drives

901
sunglasses

902
lip balm

903
reading glasses

904
board games with
magnetic pieces

905
silly string

906
butterscotch candy

907
the peace corps

908
protein powder

909
an old-fashioned soda

910
anne lamott books

911
chamomile tea

912
"masterpiece theatre"

913
corn nuts

914
fleece-lined clothes

915
ice cream sandwiches

916
hypo-allergenic soap

917

tweezers

918

teeth whitener

919

chewable antacids

920

zip-lock bags

921

smoke alarms

922

gummy bears

923

citronella candles

924

juice boxes

925

lotions for sensitive skin

926
razors for sensitive skin

927
nurses

928
an honest answer
"speak the truth –
no matter what comes of it."
ELLEN GLASGOW

929
potluck dinners

930
tiramisu

931
getting your second wind

932
integrity

933
bruce springsteen

934
new beginnings
"what the caterpillar calls the end,
the rest of the world calls a butterfly."
LAO TSU

935
a sense of purpose

936
a sense of humor

937
a plump armchair

938
creative juices

939
provocative political cartoons

940
cancer survivors

941
perspective

942

a guardian angel

943

dessert

944

insulation

945

helium balloons

946

balloon animals

947

cooperation

948

an apology

949

fond farewells

950

an umbrella

951
snow falling under a streetlight

952
shelter from the storm

953
mercy

954
miracles

955
warm sunshine on your face

956
"the chronicles of narnia"

957
harry potter

958
car pools

959
progress (even a little progress)

960

pet-sitters

961

home-grown produce

962

broadband

963

new additions to a family

964

modern medicine

965

significant others

966

our armed forces

967

unconditional love

968

healing

969
monkey bread

970
the rewards of hard work

971
priorities

972
humble beginnings

973
good sportsmanship

974
the words and example of abraham lincoln
"most folks are about as happy as
they make up their minds to be."
ABRAHAM LINCOLN

975
retail therapy

976
wake-up calls

977

gracious winners

978

competition

979

loyalty

980

an open mind

981

noble goals

982

sincerity

983

a pat on the back

984

peace of mind
"i never think of the future.
it comes soon enough."

ALBERT EINSTEIN

985
mulligans

986
teamwork

987
promises kept

988
the salvation army

989
the voice of experience

990
perseverance
"you may have to fight a battle
more than once to win it."
MARGARET THATCHER

991
a good scary movie

992
"gone with the wind"

993

an eager student

994

a patient teacher

995

a change of heart

996

online communities

997

medical advances

998

a deadline met

999

time for reflection

1000

a parking space
that opens up
right when you need it

1003
Amaryllis
flowers

1002
Hawaian
punch

1004
Best friends for life

1001

love still conquers all

If you have enjoyed this book,
Hallmark would love to hear from you

BOOK FEEDBACK
Hallmark Cards, Inc.
2501 McGee
Mail Drop 215
Kansas City, MO 64108

Or e-mail us at
booknotes@hallmark.com

a smile from a stranger 73 black-and-

328 they've finally created some energy

ips 84 texas toast 424 bendy straws 6

e north star 124 good-flavored mouthwa

07 you don't have to pretend to like forei

n actually make free throws 157 bird fee

otsie 222 friday is never that far away 2

r a streetlight 972 humble beginnings 2

mples 363 bob dylan 396 there are

444 free cell phone minutes 471 fin

eaties 527 warm, fluffy clothes and towel

arshmallows 600 a seemingly infinite su

here you really need one 856 honeybee

st base 925 lotions for sensitive skin 9